These are Zion poems chanti
the present and the future, intersecting and blending all into a
powerful song, where sisters and brothers, regardless of their
national lineage, dance in unity, ensuring a collective survival.
Monica Minott's voice rides on the shoulder of Kamau Brathwaite,
but in a distinctly Jamaican pitch that is uniquely her own.

– Opal Palmer Adisa

In her brilliant new collection, *Wandering Spirits of Exile*, Monica Minott
presents poems as a series of dialogues, conversations, arguments
and ripostes. Classical tales are subverted to the perspectives of the
"burnt face... people... of the West Nile" and there is a celebration
of the voices of the everyday and quotidian which shines through. A
stunning series of poems devoted to Jamaica's sole national heroine,
Nanny of the Maroons, offer delightful juxtapositions as when Queen
Nanny meets Chaucer at his English home. The poems are insistent
in telling these stories from the point of view of the oppressed.
Gorgeous poems dedicated to Jamaican Taíno artefacts abound,
insisting on the melding of Africa, the African and the Indigenous.
While the collection engages with the visual arts, the poems single
out the work of Basquiat, who is treated as a truly diasporic figure.
Despite the weight of history, these poems are generous, incantatory,
incandescent and enchanting.

– Jacqueline Bishop

All Praise for Monica Minott's new collection!

– Major Jackson

Winsome Minott continues her compelling exploration of Jamaican history and culture. *Wandering Spirits of Exile* identifies "archives/ of oppression" and celebrates ways of coping. After a section on colonization and slavery, there is a section on Maroons and one on visual artists, mainly Jean-Michel Basquiat (but also Kapo and Gene Pearson). The structure of the collection seems to say that artists, "hybrid", "multicultural", will show the way to Zion.

— Mervyn Morris

Whether she is inviting us to reflect on history or today — hymn or dancehall, poet, painting, or prophecy — Winsome Monica's verse is imaginatively grand, lyrically large, and profoundly wise.

— Kezia Page

WANDERING SPIRITS OF EXILE

MONICA MINOTT

WANDERING SPIRITS OF EXILE

To: Emma

Fr: Winsome Monica Minott

All that is Good
2025

PEEPAL TREE

First published in Great Britain in 2025
Peepal Tree Press Ltd
17 King's Avenue
Leeds LS6 1QS
UK

ISBN 13: 9781845235994

Supported using public funding by
**ARTS COUNCIL
ENGLAND**

CONTENTS

Section iii:
Your Paint, My Canvas

LIGNUM VITAE

"Three wooden figures (said to be Taíno deities… zemis) were put on display before the Society of Antiquaries of London."

Hardwood taking shape.
                Cacique listens to grain
                          of the wood, turns voice
                                    into form.
Ancestors' knowledge-tree bends
                but never breaks, stone-
                        chisel strips away bark
                              revealing heart-wood
ready for stone grinder.
                Bevelled liberation. Bird-
                        man finds tree-of-life
                            good to make ships.

SECTION I: ITERATIONS OF SHIPS THAT SCATTERED US

- "Between 1662 and 1807 British colonial ships [carried] an estimated 3,415,500 Africans. Of this number, around 2,964,800 survived the 'middle passage' and were sold into slavery in the Americas.

- The transatlantic slave trade was the largest forced migration in human history and completely changed Africa, the Americas and Europe.[1]

---

1. 'London and the Slave Trade, International Slavery Remembrance Day' Royal Museums Greenwich.

A PRAYER FOR SHIPS THAT SCATTERED US

May the ships that scattered us bear witness,
so that I, too, might find proximal peace.

Still searching for peace and men long dead?

May a faithful railroad track, bones of men
who never made it across (starving sailors and

Africans too sick, too weak, too troublesome)
find a margin of peace if not the whole.

Stains and shame of slavers so hard to wash away.

May continents of longing – yearning to see enemies
swallowed into the blue – be satisfied by the waves

of forgiveness, as cyclones appear mid-ocean,
on time to whip up a frenzy carrying water afar.

I have a burden for ships, yet ships have no heart!

And what of heartless men? I build seawalls
of acceptance if not understanding; only then

will each cyclone dissipate, cool down. In the
ocean of now, time, man, and magic inseparable.

Yes, the wind unnerves me, it tells me nothing.

We learn that "Prospero still fears Caliban, yes
he sees much of himself in his would-be-slave."

He begs me to transplant my black heart for
heartlessness, shed the skin of empire for ruin.

Ah, the taste of the sea still stings my tongue.

I swallow the sea's energy. I find a newborn me,
not one clothed in garments of borrowed silence.

In an evolving day, the sea — at first a frivolous
emerald-green — is forced to grow up into cobalt.

I entreat bones in the deep to put on new flesh.

Yet, what explanations do we give to our children
and their children when they question

insidious names of slavers: *Success, Satisfaction, Free Bounty?*
Each name carrying the potential of a tripwire!

LA SANTA MARIA:
KAMAU REASSESSES COLUMBUS' TRAVELS

A crumbling Rome set-off dread rumblings,
    Kamau calls it! *Not by chance Columbus sails west*

    to find east. Is a force greater than de man bring de fire
        firing up the world, a rupture launching mantu-spirits.

Columbus, a blind bat flying into daybreak,
stumbling over the seas, slipping by Daedalus' labyrinth,
invisible to the waves driving *La Santa Maria*, invisible to
a sliver of sharks moving by instinct, he sails west.

    Who fe hear hear. An irreversible landing. We who live on
        unpossessed lands, dem come fi reconfigure we footprints.

    If waters had high-spirit insight, they'd gang together and
        censure the Pinta, Niña *and* La Santa Maria.

Columbus get free pass. *Look...Armageddon!*
Who fi feel no feel yet. Dem say dem clean islands free of
aborigines. Arawaks and Caribs languishing under
sugarcane sicknesses before blue eyes turn to Africa.

    Columbus' free pass tidalectic-strong, wave after wave
        other European spectral-mantu-sprits rise. Is like spite.

    They hold continental man in triangular detention, rulers
        of earth B.C. know Columbus' route is a winding roadmap to

Armageddon!
Armageddon!
Armageddon!

We who come after, our feet searching for home, find
a crush, a carnival of bones, each day's red tint
bruising the skies. Migration ships scatter our voices. Must avoid
straits separating Africans from Africa. Time to reconnect.

MARIE SÉRAPHIQUE OF NANTES
(Channelling Kamau Brathwaite through time travel)

A slaver leaves Le Havre for Africa; next stop: a place of the have-nots —
    no language, no family, no immortelle in Sainte-Domingue.

Asymmetrical bodies wear unearned scars; death balance
    threatens life scales. We watch you break limb after limb.

Now that perspectives have changed on genocide, heart shields
    pierced, blood runs red. Natural justice is natural, yet not

constant. Remnants look at a broken flagstaff, brown like Sycorax.
    On the way a student meets a bloodied teacher.

Thoughtfulness detonates oppression and avarice; it is
    rainmaker, gamechanger, place-setter. Ashantis upset

the stage. Speak. Rattling rage and pent-up language
    of the oppressed grow loud, then *simmer, simmer down.*

We are beyond the Middle, beyond bloodshed, en route past
    domination; an active volcano belches lava,

bleaching all in its path. *It is I-self you set upon.* We
    disappear inside ourselves. *I-self ash into invisible.*

Yet we are not travelling shadows, for you've seen
    blood run like water from our veins; a changeable wind

lands ships near our equator — French Equatorial Africa.
    You claim the sulphur. Troubling winds blow ships to Haiti.

Trafficking thousands. A back-handed right, your claim
    ought to fail. 150 million extorted! Blood money!

A no-good title pass fi payment for freedom.
Bodies live through brutal landings in bewilderment.

Geography waves a white flag.
Surrender? No!

We who believed a landlocked continent to be impermeable,
woke up pregnant with Dutch, English, and French heirs.

Ancestors invisible. My fingers traverse my body touching places
that I long to call my own, but I find your marks still there.

NEW BRITANNIA
(An English slaver destroyed along the Gold Coast)

*(Kamau in conversation with "Bijago" fathers who know "The master's tools will
never dismantle the master's house", unless there is mutiny.)*

We the people of Gambia know the call
     of drums, how children come to us pure.
Yet, we must instruct: "Pass chisel, chalice, and wrecking irons."
     Silence...optional? Then and now oppressors erect
walls. Peace... optional! Then and now violence guilty.
     They hammer profits out of our bones,
wrench jazz from hollowed-out bellies. Black prayers
     ascend. They nail our feet to the reggae of wood;
cops shoot black men on doorsteps, ask questions later.
     Later. Black bodies stacked on racks in holds.
I see justice peeking through portholes judging time.
     Time. An ocean's sensibilities detect trouble.
The people of Gambia know the call, "Moses come kill
     the serpent." Children cry out. No time to wipe tears.
A malevolent sea reinvents itself; stunted men swing cat-o'-nine tails,
     cut & carve graven images on black backs.
S is the sting in songs softly breaking; monosyllables and snap-
     root-words fire up old revolt into strip down and murder of
sin-tactical systems. Head or no head, a void. Usurpers play
     black chess, unravel cold money words, injustice scales fences.
"Should words fail, strike the match," a father's swift command.
     "Perhaps ascendant ashes will make men sober."

        "Thy will be done,

        thy kingdom come."

TAÍNOS' ZEMIS HELD CAPTIVE FOR SAFE KEEPING
(Concerning Jamaican wood carvings from Carpenter's mountain, held in the British Museum)

Sirs and Madams, now talk de truth
    tell the world how you come by these,
        shame the devil with yu confession.

It was in the crossing over? I thank you Sirs and Madams,
    for thoughtful yet forked gestures; is a strange
        move unnoo mek fe protect we heritage.

First me hear seh all granny people dead off,
    wipe out good-good by raging disease.
        De record say sailors tek dem mek sport:

target-cricket – tough wood lick off man head
    with one swing. History hard fe true. Pure
        worries inna book. In black & white print.

Ship dem come and go, stir up sea like earthquake,
    shock and after-shock; a nuh likkle
        runkous unnou mek cause spirit rupture.

All this fe sure-up we education, protection, and
    spiritual enlightenment unto salvation?
        Is like yu set fe tek liberty with high-spirit.

Wanton killing of grey-back elephant fe tusks.
    Capture and divide ancestral lands – primitive lust.
        So much effort it tek fe wisdom tree grow.

Your language is mine. I'm a daughter of Ruth,
    I mek your God mine, after all, Mama navel string
        done bury here. *"Thief from thief God laugh."*

IGNATIUS SANCHO TRAVELS ON *NOBODY.*
(Sancho's voices recall his birth on a slave ship, the ship's name
unknown.)

Bloodstains mar re-integration.
Blood oozing from ma-mammy,
in her "moder-tongue" anguish.
What is me, she, dem doing here
onboard de boat, rocking me, her
nine-month-belly side to side? Me –
she, one of de 3.4 million nobodies
cast out to sea in forced migration
on colonial ships. Unnamed graves.
It was my time to come. 1729.
Sundial has no relevance, a shrill
heat visits day and night below deck,
white noise sounding. An almost visible
black woman languishing in grey pain,
with no midwife to cut her anguish, a
navel string ripped to deliver me.
Still, I came. Now, more than then,
I remember the womb of the night sky,
water breaking, a stunning cloudburst.
On a ship without a name, I came.
Mo wa, ndinabwera, Mo wa, Mo wa.
I'm the drumming of one thousand
drums. My mother died. My father
died. Twice I crossed the divide.
I'm Ignatius Sancho or I'm Nobody.

RECOVERY
(After a caricature by Isaac Cruikshank, 1792)

Kimber insists, "The negro girl must dance the deck."
    Now a fifteen-year-old girl lies dead.

I bequeath to her the ship's name, *Recovery*. I re-imagine
    a soft cry, before he hoisted her legs high.

"God, will you not keep my ankles covered?"
    Silence dulls repeated raucous laughter.

The body of a Nubian girl laid out.
    Men gather... wanting her to pay.

Ship, sun, rope, waves, mama, papa, chains.
    A piercing cry from an ocean's depth.

"But if you tell my story, I will dance and dance
    till you and I find peace."

"If you tell my story, my unwilling feet, hoisted higher
    than his sails, will be cut down."

And so the dance resumes today.

I hear the voices of morning angels singing.
    She tells them, "Bury me in the blue, blue of the sea;
bone remnants will shine like lively pearls
    as waves gather my pieces."

A WORD FROM HERODOTUS (440 BC)
(*Telemachus' Time Travel* – A Foretelling of *Henrietta Marie's* arrival)

We are the people of the burnt face,
alive west of the southern Nile River.

Telemachus, in his desperate search
for his father's secrets, travelled to us.

With the help of ten thousand winds
he carried news of times to come, of

Henrietta Marie's arrival, a ship of
witness, of dry bones weaponising

the sea. The sea hauls gold, coltan,
and ivory – no replacing sinew.

Reward or trophy? We who continue
searching for taller truths than ourselves

know that the south declines towards
our place in the setting sun: Aethiopia.

We know healing in wild trees as heavy
as gold; running mountain water

confirms value in movement; the sun
shines brilliantly on all sides of earth.

History repairs itself. It was for his mother Telemachus
ventured afar; a mother's love unfurled his sails.

Not like men who track conflict minerals – tin and tantalum –
who force children of the Congo to dig their way into hell.

They come out wearing a dull metallic shine
like used car salesmen. Glowing bodies

spark death. Yet, blood-guilty peddlers
continue buying and selling coltan.

But, oh *Henrietta Marie*, when you could
not stop their plans, you made ready to

leave 190 Africans in Port Royal – for soon
you'd meet the reefs of Marquesas.

A match made before this world began,
forcing the seas to swallow history.

WHO WILL TAME THE SIRENS?
(after John William Waterhouse's painting,
Odysseus and the Sirens, 1891)

We speak in tongues – your language;
wild, reckless winds amplify our voices.

Once we could wail you powerless
into our cove, causing your ship to

drift into the shallows, delay your
homeward journey for many years.

We quickened your quest to find beauty,
in a moment we embraced a desire to tame

a wreckless sound. Odysseus, we brought
you into subjection; a warrior having won

one battle provokes a war. Our desire
and what you deserve are often one.

They say gods control the stars, but it
was we who steadied the waves on your

return journey. Even then, Calypso and
Penelope remained distant dreams.

Just you, us, and an open sea for company,
until thunder gave you back your voice.

Only then we sent a white-crowned seabird,
with a low steady pitch, to guide you home.

PORT MARIA
(for Nourbese Philip's celebration of resistance)

I watched her sway,
calling on
ancestors,
"Ogun"
– bells ringing,
"Kibibi"
– lights flashing,
"Atabey"
– head coverings
falling
to ground.

Struggle
is not for only a
day. Day O.

Red
spattering on
white,
a bloody show.

Oh you
Ibo man,
know me –
is me you?

Oh you
Ashanti Priestess,
know me –
is me you?

Oh you, yooou
Congo warrior
restored f... from
sea bottom
bones jumping
ju ju jumping,
a a a avoid sink hole
bones s... set, settling
within lines.

Oh, if drowning
a aa ac... accidental
chains not accidental!

I watch a zemi
scatter dust
over the deck.
I call on ancestors.
I scatter light.

JOHN NEWTON'S "THOUGHTS ON THE AFRICAN TRADE" RE-STORIED

(Newton captained the ships *Brownlow* and *Greyhound,* but he is best known for writing "Amazing Grace".)

i.) I hear Granny's voice clear as day, "Is time you find Amazing Grace."

I stand behind seeing eyes and chained feet as a floundering *Greyhound* takes on water. The storm grew still. I join with waves traversing ocean currents, smell the salty sea; I stagger aboard a vessel, my body still remembering a telling sorrow. I search the ship for hope, for a sign of conviction, a contrapuntal urgency taking hold. I watch silvered eyes overlook drowning men. I smell a raw stench below. Beasts of the sea call to the dying: "*Come!*" John's conversion slow, no Paul on the road to Damascus. The sound of gold makes for deaf ears, ears not wanting to hear "Save us." Years later, a seaman's soul hears "blood-dimmed cries"... "*God save us.*" Today's headline: "A ship carrying Lamborghinis and Bentleys sank mid-Atlantic." The world takes notice. I wish we knew the names of those who passed this way. Anonymity grieves sand and sea; they are but a faded page of a ship's log. I live to live towards forgetting.

ii.) *"Amazing Grace how sweet the sound that saved a wretch like me."*
Is so I apply grace and erasure to Newton's "Thoughts on the
African Trade"

██ I first saw the Coast of Guinea in the year of our Lord 1745,
██ Disgraceful branch of commerce. ██ Trafficking. ███
Bound for the Indies. Hope this stain ████ will not ██ be
wiped out; ███ throw my mite into a stockyard ████ I piece
information together; ███ not by might, ██ by interference. ██
Necessity. ██ Bound am I in conscience to take shame, shame
to take. ████ Public confession sincere comes too late. Too late
to matter. ███ To prevent, or repair misery, and mischief. ██. No. No
mischief, ██ I'll never call starvation and drowning ██ mischief again.
But this confession ██ a feckless instrument ██ will always humiliate.
A Slave once depressed ███ the lowest degree. ██ Wretched man I
am. Yet, I've forced this fate on others. ██ My last ship to sea, ███ 1754.
Ah… divine providence ██ forced scruples on me. ████ A bout of
illness arrests. ██ Enter resignation. ██ Penitence slow but for amazing
grace.

"I once was lost but now I'm found, was blind but now I see."

iii. *"Amazing Grace"*

As we sing the captain's song,
I hear a sigh before Mary Jane asks,

"Oh, captain of *Brownlow*,
who knows the seas' swell as

well as you do, or the undertow
carrying bodies below?

Brave Captain Newton, please tell
when was your come-to-Jesus tidal

moment? Please, bold investor
in the trade, pray tell Old Jimmy

Baker, almost deaf, looking over his
eyeglass, feet turned to clay.

Jimmy afraid of moves you'll make;
afraid to close his eyes even to pray."

iv. *Oh the Piercing*

Oh Abolitionist ...Oooh, when did
you write "Amazing Grace?"

I must account for the moment;
the piercing of a soul begs

for a piercing of the body;
a crown of thorns must testify.

Now see amazing grace vessels
all lined up in a singing row.

Let us get into the truth of it. No
death rehearsals. One day is enough.

Newton refuses to answer. He bows
his head, uttering a soul-torn cry.

v. *Oh the Music Sweet*

"Amazing grace, how sweet the sound that saved…
I once was lost, but now I'm found, was blind but now I see."

Is then I hear Granny whisper, "Is so 'Amazing Grace' come.
Yet, all of we, all a we … so undeserving."

PENNING DOWN POSSIBILITIES

I am at Lookout Point, studying a body of water.
No sign of Columbus's caravels – the *Niña* and *Pinta*;
they have yielded to squaddies and squad cars, to do
the work that must be done to keep native rascals
in check – men who persist in disturbing sleepers,
who hold sessions, run pot, and dance to heavy,
thumping midnight music outside Ms. Elsie's shop.

Look, there is Caliban posing as a river bookkeeper.
The bird that attends him is a scissor-tailed sky dancer,
not a swallow. Friends have left, and Caliban counts
each departure as a failure. He murmurs, "I can't tear
myself away from wandering around eight rivers, but
I know I will never go hungry. Big sea in easy reach
and yellow-tail snapper run in abundance."

Brute-force secret police... not secret no more.
Amnesty International censured their covert operations.
The rogue team responsible for the Braeton killings
must stand trial for murder, although they and their
friends say, "No innocent man died that day." I pause
on innocence. Who is arbiter of this not knowing? Is it
they who pronounce the innocent – guilty?

Caliban looks through me, juxtaposing Taínos and Churchill's
"Rogues" and "Freebooters". Stepping closer, he whispers,
"I have a question that I've had for hundreds of years:
When Columbus set sail across the Atlantic, was he a man
of straw – without straw to sleep on?" I smile at Caliban,
glad to hear the voice of the ages. "Is it not ironic
that Columbus planted flags on soil he never tilled?"

Now, aborigines roam as spectres. I'm one such inheritor,
here to tell the tale of a Taino great grandmother, Ms. Katie,
for without her these pages would be incomplete. I walk
in her wisdom-light, sure of this day, of history's reset, when
the ruling hands of Sunak, Yousaf, and Khan, albeit brief,
grasped pens of jailers (after a nightmarish night), charging
us with writing history – the might of the pen.

THOSE WHO CAME AFTER

for Kamau Brathwaite

i.

It is
It is a task
It is a task to arrive
after *Arrivants.*

ii. *The task: carry wata to water.*

Catastrophe is no cure word.
Mama is on a special journey,
assignment – wet nurse dull
babies so they won't die.
Her own babies can't find warmth,
cut off from trees planted by
ancestors, they who travelled
through rooms of no return.
Rage. You ask about our rage,
saying rage makes us inhuman.

iii. *Seventies Man Rages – Outrageous.*

Maybe his intention was to fashion
a new man, not an outrageous wind.

Let him find warmth, not add fire to
free love under the sun's naked gaze.

Let him crawl out of his island shell,
to slit the throat of a mountain goat

caught in a thicket. We enjoy dinner.
He pours rich blood in a hole, hoping

that it will satisfy earth for another
turn, another cycle of planting and reaping.

He leaves the family to hunt alone.
Meets his match. Time so fleeting,

we learn abandonment. Slip sliding out
of despair, he dips into a communal pot,

finds ground provisions from the soil:
okras, cho-cho, potato, pepper and yam.

His hands conspire with earth. Produce.
We listen to Music of the World on the BBC,

absence blaring soft, hoping for middle C.
But the politics of the day is relentless.

I say, "Time to get tough on crime. Mind-
less shootings, seven domino-man dead.

All they want was a cold Red Stripe beer,
and to lick a double six. Thirst quencher."

Powerlessness peeps out; behind iron
gates we become "Others" at home. Cry,

cry eye-water, we hiding from devastation.
But, but wait, listen... hear catastrophe

bawl-out as it crashes to ground.
Feel it. Man and machine gun

release another sound. And is the poor, poor
people get it. Again. Time to mek a dub

plate, seal in the pain of the poor. Blood
bought lands. Our blood, your land.

We asking de governors, "Is who have
the power now?" And "Who leading who?"

iv. New Arrivants Now Revellers

Imagination cops a space in the world.
We catch at sounds and make new rhythms
that move, migrate us out of darkness.
A language-thing we-a-defend... depend on
to bring brilliant light to our shores.
Must settle the score. Ancestors watching,
wondering what we'll say when we speak.

It's never quite what you think, not revellers'
night on Kingston streets. Mojito Mondays
is where you'll find the saved, pulsing, sassy,
flirting on the outskirts of solemnity, testing
arguments of what constitutes sin, rehashing
the priest's Sunday message, his chant of love
circling like a blessed aura of grace, until the
next warm Weddie-Wednesday. Stone Love
lowers the pressure, taking night-lifers into
heavy thumping sounds, powering-up the crew,
pumping pressure against fiction. Factions
hold shady truths; life calls out, "Arrivants,
absolve self, role reversal in play.
Assignations incomplete, compete under non-compete.
On Fiction Fridays, a new man shows up,
alive in de sounds and rhythms of free."

On Saturday nights, something sinister lurks
on Kingston streets, no one sure what it is
nor when it will appear. It snakes under-
ground, like steam from an active volcano,
shifting plates. Scammers & murderers
mixed in the crowd. Catastrophe. Dress-up
uptowners and downtowners showing skin
dripping sweat to the same toasty rhythms.
Blaring sirens now one with the music.
Dancers' feet receive authority to dance.
Music shines the floor with gladness. Sad
policemen drink juice and smoke weed.
But suddenly you realise a man's scoping you
out among the crowd; eyes lock, blood runs cold.
So far so good; nobody get dead yet. Tonight.

Arrivants replay yesterday's news release:
"Scammer-duppy on the loose in Mo-bay."
"Man kill woman after she lock shop."
But this is Kingston, world-party-capital,
civilization as we know it. Governor-pirate
Henry Morgan paved the road with gold;
we inherit 10ft arrow-tipped iron gates.
We watch language ease out of innocence.

SECTION: II *TRAVELLING SPIRITS OF NANNY*

I call on you my sisters:
you who hear the sounding of drums, must fight, must dance,
must sing.

NANNY'S POT

Always boiling, frothing, ready for de enemy.
Foreigners seh, "It's a metaphorical pot, set
like turbulent waters of Stony River." But
true Maroon know better. Pot is pot, and
fire is fire, is that we talking bout. Hot fire
burn bright, no inna no mix-up, mix-up.
Fire draw dem out, unlucky British soldiers
who waaan see her boiling pot, dem creep-up
behind almond tree. Maybe is brew call them,
but as soon as them draw close, dem collapse.
Maroon seh, "No explanation necessary, cause
Nanny nuh pay nobody no mind. Every enemy of
Nanny is an enemy of pot and fire." Nanny
leave it to the pot, pot leave them to fire.
Pot draw them come, Nanny sort them out.
Mpoto abweletse. Moto! Moto!

BUCK TOE STONE

(Story of the offending stone published in the *Jamaica Daily Gleaner*, 16 October 2021)*

Is so Maroon become visible again.
After many years of salting self away
from the public gaze, as chance would have
it, on an ordinary day, a quiet sojourner
travelling uphill buck him Portland toe.

Buck-toe summon an agitated army
to my not-so-small acreage to prove Nanny!
As if Nanny need proving. The stone had the
stamp of British invaders. Is language give
dem wey after four hundred years in hiding.

"This town was held by Capt. Cook till July 2nd 1735."
"Held! Is who do the holding?" I stomp the stone!
I dance the stone! Talk to uncle the beekeeper who
tarry further uphill – is him know bout Nanny. "She
never swallow her spit, always moving stones."

Nanny is protector of secrets, is woman, is preacher, is hero.
While we anxious to keep invisible, Nanny come and go as
she please; no skipping over transgressions, she tests hot coals.
English fe tek shade.

MAPPING THE POLITICS OF WE, US & THEM
(for Dionne Brand)

We honour ancestors with sage,
anoint ourselves with jasmine.
Is it possible to disaggregate "we",
to disarm Babylon's infidels who
strong-arm government temples
in the name of progress? Bloodied.
Our hands less valued than the blood
of spotted goats and rams. We refuse
to join lines for handouts, refuse to
take dispossession for granted. This
makes for sadness, so we catch on the
red crabs' annual trek back to the sea.
We who restate terms of occupation
know when we = *them*, they give us
old names, give us a lesser place.
Know when we = change, we ask
for a-right-fix. We speak life as we
redesign the fate of the planet.

For we who have been confined to
covid-crawl spaces know time is
challenging us, expanding we – a
valid establishment, forcing a white
contingency into our black spaces,
hollow holdings, zoom-room-screens.
Grief makes us all vulnerable to light.
Yet, we are all called to survive,
ought to synthesize all previous
encounters, shift configurations
dividing us, embrace we-wisdom.
There will be no return to normal.
The way to keep geography alive

is against the door of no return —
four hundred years — against tens of
millions shackled and trafficked.
We re-map old routes,
hold sacred de strength of a woman.

We look to Queen Nzinga,
Nanny of the Maroons,
Queen Mother Nana Yaa Asantewaa,
Queen Zewditu, Katherine Henry,
Ethel Edwards, and Ignota Elouise for clues,

understanding the world of "we" and "us"
is stronger than "they" or "them". If we do
not listen, the world will teach us again
and again. Connectivity. It's ultimately
about drizzle and the rain, lion and lamb,
volcanic mountains, oceans, continents,
islands, human-kind and kindness.

NANNY SLEEPS UNDER A BROOM TREE

The day Nanny lay down and sleep under a blossoming
broom tree was a day just like today. She never get up
for many moons. A smell of honey stirs aching bones;
she finds an unconventional meal: warm exile bread.

Nanny don't know how she arrive in the desert; she travel
far and had further to go. Yes, she get a call to show up
in the land of wood and water, Xamayca! She dusts sand
and fire embers from the bread, then put it to her lips.

A muscular wind came, mountains trembled, a voice said:
"Faith is not in the wind." After the wind, an earthquake.
"Faith is not in the earthquake." The earthquake spat fire.
"Faith is not in the fire." Only in that still small voice.

"Shake off sleep-stupor." Nanny catch His voice. "No badda hide,
mi girl." Nanny rubs her eyes, rubbing out perplexing sand.
This earth journey hard fe true when man haffi battle man.
But the voice said, "Get up, chile, return yourself to born place.

Cockpit country never short of a blessing. Claim it, tek
land fe language and language fe land." Nanny tek de stick
mark out a legacy in the topsoil. Cudjoe come and gone
Quao time come and gone… is my time, is your time!

A strong wind broke the mountains.
A voice said, "Belief is not in the wind." And after the wind an earthquake.
"Belief is not in the earthquake." The earthquake spat fire;
"Belief is not in the fire." Only in a still small voice. Imagine.

"Which self will rise tomorrow?" No certainty. Sacrifice.
In the land we find de future, we bury our past. Call out
with cow horns and seashells, beat back overgrowth
with macka sticks, till prickle talk back to you hand.

Blow de horn — no not once, maybe seven times seven.
Sound de sweet ole-talk, our language; dance sideways
till a brighter morning come. Click heel and toe to ground.
Ruckumbine, rock and come in. Nanny is conqueror!

DANCEHALL MUSEUM

My body is never still. There is no deception in
movement. It is a call and response to archives
of oppression; no food to eat deep in the ghetto.

This is where I come to set my troubles down –
on a dance floor, on a pavement, on any table
strong enough to hold the weight of memories.

My body is never still; there is no deception.
One with a drumbeat, I am like burning wood
in a backyard furnace, red as blood memories.

This is where I come to lay my troubles out,
in the spirit of dancehall, wine, twist, a jook –
body-loud. Cease and settle. We have rhythm.

Drums deliver notification; my body receives
initiation. Blood messages travel my veins,
shouts of exultation assault nerve endings.

Out of the bowels of the deep deep ghetto,
agile born-ready bodies gyrate, releasing
words and prescriptions. Boomshackalaka.

We never repeat stories once told – break down,
reconstruct, punctuate, hips spinning out syllables;
words fall from my lips before they hit ground.

Words take the shape of my spine and ass-ets.
Spirit of dancehall alive in the wine, twist, and jook.
We belong. In community no defeat. Resistance.

This is my body – a top notch museum.

NANNY SPIRIT TRAVELS –
SUPPLIANT SISTERS

Spirit marks in Argos predate movements in
Ghana, predate Nanny Town, "specterrific!"

Nanny, always a freedom fighter, crisscrossing
oceans, moving swiftly across boundaries.

No bush nor fire can detain spirit; geography
is her way over – she fashions new pathways

mapped in her head. No scouting detail can
locate Nanny's tracks when she decides to hide

herself in the bosom of "*I-self.*" She vanish!
The evidence resounding in the *Pata Pata*

of Makeba's songs, in each touchdown –
guerrilla territory. Breeze-blow British men

would rather be dead than meet Nanny
along her flying zinc-leaf banana track.

The day Nanny tun up in Cockpit Country,
we who understand know that spirit-work

must go on. Mek no mistake, woman
work nuh done till lionheart of freedom

ketch and mark her as her own – big woman.
I watch de Nanny-spirit boomerang like bullets.

Patches of cultivated ground near each hut
confirm survival as resistance.

Bump Grave marks one cycle. Time out!
Yu-day-done! Nanny spirit-work just begun.

MAPPING MAROON TERRITORY

Co-ordinates to find me is not for
        John Public to see, but if you can
  keep haphazard a secret, *wheel and come in*.

      Nanny Town:18.0683°N 76.5242°W
Charles Town: 18.2242° N, 76.6622° W
  Moore Town: 18.0723° N, 76.4254° W.

All three bush sanctuaries lie deep
      in the airy hills of Portland. Scotts Hall,
sweeping the border, is home for we who refuse fi live

      under a thumb of oppression. Vow:
"Freedom or death in Father's land!"
  We who live in these hills practice to

  dodge the bullets, never walk in a
      straight line, know river rising is a
certain way to escape plunder. Climb.

      Father forgot the many secrets downriver.
  He fell for the thundering arms of a city.
I'm making my way up-mountain to safety.

SPIRIT OF JONKONNU REACH THE LANE

Christmas time near when the red peas buss him shut, and Aunty tek down
her Home-Sweet-Home lamp, trim the wick and shine it up clean.

— after Fae Ellington

Till the music of a Jonkonnu band reach your lane,
and you see picknie hold tight to Mama's skirt,
just in case they haffi hide, is not Christmas.
Goat-skin drums carry the first gust of sound,
six bunches of green bananas and two plantains
shimmering, ackee spirit walks with sweet yam,
watermelon and ginger never far behind. "Man
must have spirit to live," while Pitchy Patchy
still twisting and turning like pitchy-patchy.

ii)
Emancipation streets always overcrowded.
Every jack man, woman, and child dress
to forty-nine. Sound system on a break;
a lull signals something big soon come.
A float led by Bad Gal Nanny and Bad Boy
Marcus encourages freedom and good sense.
"No hostage here, we come fe get a job done," Ms
Nanny cry out. But Mavis (an ole timer) on mi right,
keeps mumbling, "When will the killings stop
to let us know we are free?"

iii)
"But kiss me neck, this band travelling with
two devils and two Horseheads." Two devils
shake fists at the crowd. The crowd, having
grown accustomed to mayhem and massacre,
did not budge. A few men under de whites
mock the devil, and one young man try
to run down Horsehead to get a free ride.

"Signs of times to come," Nanny said.
"Murder no nothing," Ms Mavis chided.
Perhaps we need drink sinkle bible and beg
politicians in government to trim the size
of the Jonkonnu bands. We don't need two
devils nor two Horseheads. Nanny talk truth.
"Is better the country not even have one."

COLOUR "I" DANCEHALL
(after Ebony Patterson's *Dead Treez*)

"What to make of it?
Yellow-framed glasses lighting on high fashion moves,
living shout-out to energy packs, salutations to the sun.
I pick a sunflower – or am I the sunflower, kotching
stage right? Am I spinning, or is a moving
stage spinning me round and round?" A Kingston posse
appears. Their finest hour. "Who goes there?"

"Is only I and I"... a whisper barely audible, "Careful,
Patterson arrests even the dead. She better than night noise-
police-officer who bawl out *Freeze!* Any dancer who is
an inch from the floor better hold that position – less Corpie,
who waan earn two stripe, fire in earnest at the slightest
movement. I caan forget when penny drop on Lennox's
dancehall groove, he catch *yellow pages* in a secondary

wine, dancers feet spread before the lift and flip."
"I vow to uplift dancehall." No mistaking a subversive plan.
"But de people nah dance," a casual passerby droned. "Gangstas
don't dance dancehall as you imagine. Look, colours on busy
duty: reds, blues, greens, yellows – calling on earth's varied
flowery routines. Blacks, whites, pinks – adopting harmony's
twists and turns; zig-zag bites getting up on down patterns,

I and I conspire with shades of irregular."
"Yes, eye-catching in their own pitchy patchy way." Some
moving cool to a Jam-swag, others with a Brazilian
carnival shuffle. "It took a while for the 'I' to *peni*
the pink and white polka-dot skin, brown patches
grafted on black faces, many multi-coloured hybrids
left over after colonial occupation and bleaching."

"But here we are after frantic yellow fever and covid.
Still someone dares tell me what to wear, how to lean,
when to dance. I say, *Hello! I'm mellow in my pink-
and-black checkered diamond jumper, you in your
red, black, and gold striped jacket. A cover.* Floral
ghetto vest tests a stand-out green pants." Posse
caution, "Murderous colours catch dancing feet."

NANNY AS CRITIC AND THE CARIBBEAN QUARTET

To be clear, the Redcoats were no more
than peenie wallies in Cockpit country; they

had no business in bush-business. Yet,
maybe is them bring-out the best in Nanny

and dem other hill soldiers like Quao, who
never afraid to dress down the first-catch;

remove the red coat, and everything else
and watch the others chase downhill like

fire deh a muss-muss tail. Don't ask me
why, but red coats remind me of poets

carrying business cards – on that I've been
schooled. Their only trade is word-for-word

and metaphor for metaphor, so we agree
to disagree, argument never done! Long

day-metre follow night, Lamming name it
"the quarrel", and V.S. Naipaul, that carry-

down-artist, shame us again and again,
say we know nothing, and we is nobody!

I watch Walcott back-off him shirt and
draw for the pen; he'll not have meters

maligned, is only then the quarrel get
red, so much so, Baugh decide it was

time to put in waterways, roads, signs
and borders to contain the language

of "history" and "historylessness." Is so
Caribbean literary landscape draw.

To be clear, is critics shine light
on the legacy, for I don't know

what would happen if Nanny never
tek Redcoat and make pillow at

every tree root she sleep. When
morning come, she bury them same

place, a subversive promise made.
So, when you look uphill and see red

twinkling in the sunlight, the flame
of the forest is but a witness, trying

to deliver as Nanny delivered — her
fire and fury as high-warning.

WORDS ON A SLOW BURN

"There're things I must tell you about how I am feeling."
"No, do not tell me," the poet said. "Show me." Today was
an unusually cold day for October. I remember shifting,
positioning my body near to a burning flame. *How do I
show a wordsmith cold and heat in one go?*

I grew quiet, not wanting to sound silly. I thought of
ways I might transform ice to vapour in a millisecond,
but none seemed satisfactory. Then I knew he was
being clever, that old goat. He was telling me he
wanted more than a long road at the journey's end.

I asked, "What has changed? I am still a woman
in exile, away from my country, away from many
things that I love." "But you are here now," he plainly said.
I nodded. "Metaphors are overrated," I said. He smiled.
We had little choice; we let a slow burn begin.

PROCLAMATION: 1ST AUGUST 1834 FREE PAPER GRANT

*"...all and every person who on the said first day of August one thousand
eight hundred and thirty-four ...be to all intents and purposes free and
discharged of and from all manner of slavery, and shall be absolutely and
forever manumitted."*

Enacted,

    not enacted,

        all slaves

            every single one a dem shall

kuwa,

    become

        free! Discharge from a charge

        manumitted,

1834 to 1934

    no enactment,

        no home: no land, no language, no voice,

            we've come full circle.

A call, a call,

    free the mind.

        Permit grant, pass de abeng.

August morning, centre of centre.
Only we, you and me, can, must
remove from our necks the yoke;
a blistering heaviness remaining
after the proclamation is read;
August morning welcome de spirit –
broken tongues. No forgetting...

Absolutely,

kabisa,

from then

recover voice and language –

not become,

not become,

said day

free, yet not free. Intent subverted –

time lost –

revaluation –

in the present.

Black intent and black purpose –

moving on.

Restatement.

Silent remembrance.

Never forget the proclamation.
Provoke de purpose of redress,
no-redress-faulty. Free by birth –
certain. Man-made exploitation –
un-read a faulty decree. Proclamation
spirit stretches to sea. No resolve –
freedom tests the depth of vision.

FRAGILE
(after Johnson Chua's photo of a kingfisher)

i)

Hear me sing till spirits find home,
I have no time, no space to think fragile.
Fragile. I am running uphill, keeping pace
with bold. I love a kind, welcoming world.
I hope to find grass when I fall, not stones.
Rain-green hills ahead, steadying Maroon
bush steps left in me, I track faint footfalls.
Digs reveal broken bones of history.
I remember when a flying fish broke surface,
swimming upstream, devouring time. Time
allows obstacle-course runners a place.

I discover caves and gorges, hear a rushing
cool, the powerful raindrops of Portland. I
never choke on the meaning of fragile.

ii)

Salting arrivals. Aboriginal tribes suffer death.
Traces of a bloodline, thin but not invisible. I
hop, skip, and jump, trying to avoid hearts cut
from stone. I sing, tether myself to ska music.
Crisp reggae leaves mark my way forward.
I accept the path a knowledge run takes.
I hear the dark cantering; it's time to leave
caves of my ancestors, make good of gifts
received – wind instruments, and bone flutes.
I lift a conch shell to my lips; a rushing
bugling sound courses downriver.

An instrument of praise. I tune a shell
to deliver a perfect sound after seventeen
thousand years. Reified. The sound is cure.

iii)

Begin again with morning, when bugling
birds, starved of flight, grow impatient
for torrential rains to cease; soon, they'll
be away. They have had enough. Enough
of mankind. Not one surviving Carib, nor
Arawak, on the running trail. Traceless.
"Are you out there?" I must run the race
set before me. Alone. I cannot be Nanny –
face of the Maroons. She is gone. My time
to add to a sprouting frail freedom story, an
evolving trail acknowledging Creole tongues.

"Fragile yet fierce?" I lean into sounding
liberation trumpets. I catch rhythms of
free, as a kingfisher perches on a lotus leaf.

MY WILD WOMAN SINGS TOO
(After "The Revival Song of The Wild Woman" – Lorna Goodison)

My wild woman has occupied headlands and straits,
circled Blue Mountain Peak, and has come head to
head with Bullhead Mountain; but my wild woman
is not your wild woman. She strings bleeding gold

around the necks of warriors, hears abengs circling,
sounding her out of deep sleep to gatherings of fighting
men, to stave off another attack from tarnished soldiers. One
more day under the fierce sun, "limbs remember bodies".

My wild woman now encourages me to write poetry,
but does not expect ballads or sad Sankeys
streaking across the night sky. She tells me:
Love only one man. Forget past lovers
who tore at my heart. Let them fall by the wayside
like seeds that fell on stony ground –
bursting through seed coats, without roots.

Rain. Summoned from the past to claim the future,
she travels through Dry River country. Thirsty,
she stopped at Flint River to drink an ice-cold dragon stout.
She is making her way to the giving land of Ethel and Ignota,
grandmother and mother. But first she must stop in Kingston
to gift me with seeing eyes of the ancestors.

I've tasted the salt and pepper of the past. I know
secrets: green healing fingers, the strength of ganja
soaked in white rum, and roads to safe passage. Port Maria's
rivers flow down a lush green hillside.

No small thing when time meets revelation; we agree
to de-colonize history. Praise all mountain songs of
Cudjoe and Nanny, claim them as knowledge. River-
consciousness leaves many baffled, yet stronger.

My wild woman agrees with your woman on one thing:
"Our enemies will never live long enough to defeat us."
Having sucked the salty sea, having drunk the sweet
of Sweet River, having tasted tamarind mixed into

new lines of poetry, I grow providential. I collect
fragments that provide shade words for children –
they who claim the coffee beans ripening on the
weathered land of Nathaniel, son of a Maroon.

CHAUCER HOUSE
(Chaucer's bones lie entombed at Westminster Abbey)

I did not set out to find Chaucer's house,
but here I am – on the landing, back against
years of turbulent trials that stormed through

      this door. At first glance, it could
      be any other old, stained-oak door.

Can't say why Ms. Nanny appears here
on the cold steps at four in the evening,
when a frozen sunset shows a glimpse of

      orange and pink. Another life assails me;
      she wishes me to share her "pot" and "fire".

Is full time they acknowledge bushmaster
and Maroons, for dem drogue us far in ship belly
to dry land and dry peas, here to there to here.

      Plant us like breadfruit tree in the West Indies.
      "Ahh, Ms. Nanny, to be politically correct we say the
Caribbean."

Hush you mouth, you just come;
everybody talking except Geoff. Is why him so silent?
Geoff, give us savages a word nuh, not only a groan.

      "What savages?" *You must learn your history.*
      No wonder Geoff groaning, little light passing.

"Maybe him contract sickness in cold Poets' corner."
Hmmm, him poem dem not too bad. You know Bump
Grave in Portland? "Yes," I replied. She nodded.

There I roam in sunshine and rain, no stained
glass windows, no Royal pension required.

And further, in your petition to
powers higher up, maybe they'll ship his
bones to Bump Grave with reparation gold.

Lots of space on the hillside; he can write
plenty poems, and I will teach survival skills.

SECTION III: MY PAINT, YOUR CANVAS.

Jean-Michel Basquiat reveals diasporic concerns and movements. He incorporates bones, skulls, ladders, his tools to enable crossing us over.

Mallica "Kapo" Reynolds explores the essence of life via nature and imagination: rocks, water, flying tables, and trees.

Gene Person's self-portraits reveal an ongoing search for self.

WARRIOR KING

(after Jean-Michel Basquiat's painting *Warrior, 1982**)

My asymmetrical body holds
stories; my right arm is Haitian,
complicating Toussaint's sword.
My left arm gangly, without a song.
I ran into a streak of good luck – a
joint inheritance flying the flag of
exploitation: *hold down and tek wey,*
a history of interbreeding. At sea
I continue fighting hybridity; knees
disjointed, bones non-aligned, I float
like driftwood. A left-seeing eye dull.

Nonapologetic. My brain connects
to ladders, stairways to heaven.
Amazing so many survive.

SITTING ON TOP OF A PAGODA
(after Jean-Michel Basquiat's painting *Pyro, 1984*)

They create a frame called terror.
I live here. I spray-paint the frame;
light creeps in showcasing breakable
bones, bent out-of-shape bones. Taking
a step back, I examine a red rocket
where my heart socket should be.
A hungry lioness guards a ticking rock.
I find trees growing out of my breast.
I hear birds nesting in-between leaves.
A red owl travels with songs of rain.
Yet all around me lie mad weapons
of war. I hide a rocket inside the
frame – a stand-in leg. My right leg
got hit in a drive-by. My friends died.
It was then I swallowed the Pagoda.
I can't understand schizophrenic English.
It had me on the run. "Run!" I heard
a shout. "Run!" I ran into my shadow
leaving millions. I'm worth more dead.
Had I remained alive, I'd tell you,
"Know your pills, never swallow a Pagoda."

BASQUIAT ACQUITS HIMSELF WITH A JAWBONE
OF AN ASS
(after, Jean-Michel Basquiat's painting *Jawbone of an Ass, 1982*)

Is Bob check me at the gate, slapped my back
and called me brother. I had to explain myself.
I was no slacker like dem from the other tribes.
I watch dem set a multitude of hurdles inna I path,
as if someone want fe hinder I. I vision the rake,
so de obstacles dem set doan even bada de I.
One by one, I cross over into the Promise Land.
Dat is how I get I gold crown, channelling gold-
talent while black. I paint an invisible ladder. I
cross over the chasm. I slay dem Philistines
when them think they safe. I hold no gun. No,
only the jawbone of an ass and one miracle.
A spray-pan with slaying powers. For real. I
see I face in the moon, a warrior sent to slay.
Pass me de jawbone with teeth intact.

BASQUIAT'S DELUSION

I am an apprentice to colour,
to dismantling my father's soul.
I give expression to error: a spider's
web, wind, grey, fog, and hurricanes.

I make it back home before
gangsters come out; splitting
coded colours ain't like hijacking
a parked car, it takes more time.

I learn how to cut the light
shading the sacrifice. Madonna
tied me to the stake. A ram is the
preferred animal. But a goat kid

knows the words I want to say;
I never imagined a world where
fragments could displace bones.
I capture ice splinters in black &

white, a spider eating his prey. I
lay me out in green pastures; they
say I'm delusional because I choose.
I choose to blunt resistance,

to silence rhetoric of sketchy men,
they who'd sideline my prints,
fictionalize my presumptiveness.
I harbour no dread delusion. Life

does not always send good rain.
Sometimes the flood overtakes
the land, calling me out to paint
tsunamis without rainbows.

DEFACEMENT

(after Jean-Michel Basquiat's *Defacement, 1983*)
– for Michael Stewart

Mama said, "If only walls could talk!"
I made it my business to speak for Mama.
The day I heard a name echo, bouncing off
walls – "Spray-painter Michael Stewart dead...
guilty of defacing the underground." *The place*
I spray-painted last week? Sticks and stones
come break my bones, could have been me.

Mike's death darkens newsstands.
Guilty only by association... *Mike my friend,*
my voice trailing off. Looks of displeasure
stifling me. *All he did was validate verse.*
A violation. East-Village-Underground was
home-for-all-homies. Our intention –
to educate, never violate. He was the pulse

of our people: travellers, fortune tellers
coming or going – never sure who to tell.
Never knew he'd be going, ooh so soon.
Spray painters have no union; a guilty law
acquits men in blue. "In the line of duty!"
"He slipped and fell!" Toes unable to grip
ground? *Damn them to the pages of hell!*
"No excessive force?" *Yet he is dead.*

So it was in 1771, Collingwood shouting:
"Man Overboard!" I watch you drown.
I tell you, brother, it could have been
me. Now they want me to beg for your
bones. But your bones are my bones. I
carry our loss, it could have been me!

FOREIGN POLICY WRITER

(Sonnets of discontent after Jean Michel Basquiat's *Eroica, 1988*)
Basquiat responds to an advertisement, "Vacancy for Policy Script
Writer, Qualification: A Life lived."

No prefix, no suffix, no degree
annexed to a life lived. How to value the
sum of sun years, be it ninety, sixty or twenty-
seven? Having joined the "twenty-seven club",
I believe I've talent enough to season lines, to
communicate livity. Foreign-minded people
and "bruck-spirit" regulators know foreign is a place
to go or not go. Yet, when you go, I'll capture
circles of your exclusion and invisibility.
Paint is my language; I have given up on
Creole, they call it bad English, cause they
don't know the root of the words spoken. Yet
want me to believe in that old woman who
lives in a shoe, her only way out is migration.

Praise ye who battle a colonizer's language.
I read in your eyes pools of survival: *Dutty
tough*, ground hard to plant, harder to reap
what has been planted. *Eroica*, morning glory
brittle like stone, *Eroica*. And so my lips,
having sucked the grapes of wrath, wear a
purple tint. Tears of joy flow. I'm a colourist.
A good cry can wipe any slate clean of false
teachings and misgivings. I offer a blank page
on which we will write a new foreign policy:
"Love yu country and love yu neighbours.
Let distractions fall to the ground. Surround
yourself with 'livity'." Come greet refugees,
give them all safe landing.

We watch weary sea legs off-board
carrying "whys" and "wherefores" too long
held – legs created for nation-making, tired
after the journey, remembering their first
disenfranchisement, dispossessed of their
lands in another century. I thread myself
through bones of found bones, acceptance.
I replace discontent with joyful colours.
A paleontologist at work fits findings in
triangles, circles, and squares. I find that
needle in a haystack; I sew skulls to crowns,
with hope that one will prick a conscience
awake, translate distorted lines into images
as I hammer out life's stony meanings.

UNDISCOVERED GENIUS
(after Jean-Michel Basquiat's painting *Undiscovered Genius, 1983*)

My toe tag reads *Genius*. A simplification.
Young and Wild stickers on my bareback.
My dreads say *Rough handle. Babylon!*

Price of colour blood-thin; a bidding
war ensues long after I have ditched
palette and designer brushes dripping

blackness, sparking controversies! "No
more where he came from. His Mama
sports red lipstick, till a smudge came.

They put her away." Unforgiving! Mama's
blues they never quite understood. Yet, I've
hugged trees, I've roamed among dragons

and bulls. "He walks the deep south at night."
I don't have to be a Mississippi Negro to know
what race feels like. I have witnessed tree-riots.

Bats come out in their numbers; seeing eyes
tell me all I need to know. I gnash tongue
across teeth, till my time frame collapses.

Dem no know seh I sit inna de uppa-room!
"A story told, traffickers stuck in a hellish ditch,
bones in bottom of ships. Ships line sea-bottom."

I bury the last sickle, axe, and fork found
aboard the last slaver bound for Mississippi.
Griot, still on my way to that place

called free. Oh, Babylon! I present I self.
Not enough images! You want more? More
self-portraits emblazoned on bags and boots?

My crown adorns dirty sneakers, ground
absorbing body parts: a head, a torso,
my heart they'll cut out tomorrow! No.

MAKING FUFU
(after Kapo's painting *Making Fufu* 1981)

For years, *Making Fufu* hung over my head –
man in field, woman pounding cassava. Pestle.
At a glance, nothing amazing about the scene;
work is as natural to man as sweat is to bread.

Press is essential in making Fufu; with each
thrust, earth colours deepen. The wind stirs an
irrepressible survival – a woman's back against
a tree wall, her thoughts – livity etched.

Kapo's colours speak in fluid alignment,
canvas statements: tall calabash trees, gushing green
vegetation fed by underground tributaries.
He preserves wild heartlands, wings of history.

Kapo claims insight — he unshackles silence,
releases water from rocks. I watch the sun light
fuchsia blooms on a bougainvillea nestling between
bottle-green privets, offset by lime-green parakeets.

Together they call on me to retrace fifty
years of mornings and four hundred years of
toil. My feet still hit ground running; I must
gallop miles till sun gives way to night-time,

and night to rest. After sweaty cotton shirts
are shed, the warm scent of sunlight hangs
in the air, lingering among bedcovers –
spent bodies ripe in the peace of before-light.

"What lines can challenge a painting hanging
on a wall?" Perhaps a crusading heart shaping
futures, a mother and daughter duo, father and
son breaking bread. Love, love, and more love.

Yes, struggles continue into wee hours of morning,
hairlines thin and smells diminish. Today I call on
willing hands still strong. I pound cassava.
"Today I'll make Fufu."

A REVIVALIST GOING TO HEAVEN.
(after Kapo's painting with the same name, 1968)

Is not the first time you spin you taste glory.
There is God and good in each rotation. Earth
knows the drill; mark your spot, let light overtake
each turn, feel each tilt of the axis shaping a body
in motion. It is "catch, cleanse, and release."

Is not the first time you catch the sway —
that you sense the presence of the all-knowing spirit.
Every dancer worth them salt can testify, don't
need no sprinkling of white rum fi ketch dance
fever; a sounding drum is more than enough.

The Master Drummer's presence is inviolate.
I am, because of the I Am, in need of no special
introduction; only praise and worship songs
and trained feet certainty can enter into His
presence, into "catch, cleanse, and release."

Revival assumes a groundswell. Unlearning
chaos leaves space to learn the rhythm of drums.
Drumming anchors one as eternity is poured in.
I ease into understanding, all I should know
when that sobering light like a bird comes

to sit on my shoulder. On that revival day
ready hearts will open to a great refreshing
as turbaned heads look to the sky. See Kapo's
gifted imaginative bird-angels fly — ready
to ferry souls across the finish line.

ROCK-STONE ARTIST
(after Kapo's painting *Treasure Rock Faces*)

I born, I draw, I paint, I carve, I write.
Oh… you my blessed, I chisel high cheek-
bones, and carve flintstone-seeing eyes.

Your light carries light many moons –
high-blue. Eternity. Silver draws me
out. I fly. A tricky flight of feelings.

I born, I draw, I paint, I carve, I live.
My blessed stirs in me calabash stories,
capturing cobalt seas; I watch as seas collide.

Grey eyes and a provocative smile, a signal.
Yet, you would not stay, could not stay.
I chiselled you beautiful. Rock-of-ages.

I born, I draw, I carve, I live, I die.
O blessed sentences. O rock, separated from
a forever mountainside, I rework pigments into

stony indentations, calling on colour – enigmatic,
every fibre of you. I watch eager stones grow into
Mt Zion's trovants. "Maybe in another lifetime,

you and I." I born, I draw, I paint, I carve. Today
I name you faithful, a keeper. In my rock-stone
world, I'm alert to energy. Timelessness.

GENE PEARSON'S MASKS
(Gene Pearson's *Bumpy-Head Gal*)

My first mask… no more than a rustic mojo.
Early journeys spin deep. I imagined a glazed
metallic mask with a shine as mine. Impostor.

After days of wrist-circling alkaline variations,
self-proud, I wore no armour of conceit, no acid
pretensions rasping against clay. Lean fingers

learn to decipher varying grades of grain, the
voice of each grain telling. A good outcome is
he who never forgets the science of his making.

A few masks lie dormant for years, readying
for the David moment. Time arrives unbidden
when purpose unfolds as a surprise.

Yes, even the selves whose feet are made of clay
will find a top-mask to worry all imaginations
afresh, as aged dreams conspire with reality.

The bumpy-head gal echoes one voice of clay,
proud, resilient, no nonsense, *nah tek no fool-
fool talk from nobody*; she projects change.

A green mask, sporting cornrows and a wide mouth,
swallows my right hand – releasing me only after
Patwah and I talk as friends. No kiss-teeth.

Salted handprints mark a golden-glazed mask.
Perhaps heat cures mouldy maladies. Revelation. I've
travelled through fire and I've tasted river-water.

I've willed rain to lift Creole vessels aright, as dub
sounds conspire with winds, thunder, and the sun
to return salt to the sea. The sea washes my feet.

I fire-up each wound of clay. Courage arrives on
a Monet's sunrise. Dormant masks snatch at life. I hear
voices. *Nah tek no fool-fool talk from nobody.*

ZION, WHERE SEA MEETS SKY

We will meet again, by way of the sea,
Mt Zion Hill, a high place of higher calling.
Katie turns clay to make yabbas,
provoked by rushing dawn winds
raising her up to touch ancestors
in Ethel's born place.

We wrestle giftings, hand-me-downs.
Come bless me, oh benevolent rain. It's hard
not to love your blooms – growing wings
while grace pots and yabbas make ready
to show-off "daylight splendor".

And so we approach each new bend
in the road… cautious, knowing that
born-again giftings, like the flower of
a coratoe, will dream us into fullness.

ii)

The salting of a yabba, brown earthenware vessel,
is a lesson travelling across intrepid waters in search
of justice: fired-up clay, turned, polished, cooled.

In time yabba confounds a Spanish jar, infiltrator
hedging golden promises. Not much left here – only
fragments washed ashore; imaginings, soundings
dipping and heaving against mountains of lives,
settling in between cracks. A flower opens to
earthsounds as morning renews itself and folds,
while nighttime lulls tired legs to sleep. I gather
fragments – naming ships that scattered us.

iii)

In my corner, a fragile yabba pot rests its
heel, contemplating a gathering together.
Beside the yabba, a circle reserved for the missing.
So many have left us, leaving behind untold stories
growing in cracks and crevices.

A locator search ensues, the Spanish jar
        holds tense rhythms of voices
irretrievably lost in a thicket. We hear

chirping crickets, we rely on Mama's notes
        to make strong Katie's survival, in a time
past yet present.

Seals I crack open, multicultural in
        dimension. Tainos appear
in my sisters' steps, in my daughter's stories,

in family paintings. In this way,
        I've become hybrid. Culture becomes us,
artists longing for Zion.

iv

And so they divided us like cattle, they cut out our tongues to
prevent rebellion, yet the lineage of artistry survives. I call you
Sister, you who hear the sound of drums and must dance. I call
you Brother, you whose gifting is made complete as you work
in acrylic and oils, as you draw on the energies of ages past and
of times to come – you who channel the sun's eye as you mould
willing clay into form. I meet a stranger, man not of my tribe,
yet his saxophone is witness that perhaps we are one stock, after
yellow fever, after cracked skulls. Severed fingers and toes, having

fused to new bodies, offer up new identities, never complete.
Dust-covered terrains are now submerged in the depth of an
ocean. Yes, we evolve. The artist in us
keeps repeating in every generation.

v)

Today's moth-eaten skies arrive, bending
into a horizon like an apology, replacing
fast-moving dark clouds of misgivings.
I'm ready to give way, step over blankets
of smoke; it is here, in "in-between" spaces
I am most uncertain. Ethel, child of
Busha and Kathrine, is proof that Carib
blood disappears downstream —
overtaken in the wash of two continents.

One story remains fluid:
        the river carrying the tale of a lost
                Spanish jar. Earth-brown clay

re-shaped, polished to shine
        trimmed in cracked spaces, trace
                metals and gold cooling.

As children, we've had the joy of "Blow Hole"
        till the likes of Ian Fleming buy-out Aunt Gwen's
Oracabessa property for cheap cheap.

Campbell land tek time dwindle down,
        but we remember idyllic summers,
crayoning names on warm rocks,

our small bodies, immersed
in blue-emerald-green warm water,
till waves drown the sun's daily allotment.

We walk at a steady pace, returning to a sea
path travelled by Katie, we imagine her
soldiering motion, her movements timeless.

Along the hillsides we'd count coratoe
blooms for luck, maybe one agave
root is the keeper of great-granddad's secret.

vi)

No British air for me today, when
it is grey and hung low – like Massa
after he has scored one too many.

The air is thick with rain, yet it will
not fall. I see your body as you once
saw Black bodies landing on UK shores –
incidental. Maybe I'll be useful after
fresh paint marks me as an Arrivant.

Know, when we land, we require no
special occasion to celebrate; we wear thorns
in a land of confused outcomes.

Yet, you'd extract the horn of blackness
the essence of the Coratoe saved up
for that spectacular inflorescence show.

Maybe you should
suffer the same fate as you lie
here curled, spooning my body.

Yet all we long for is justice,
        we, who are born old. Until then, let us
                fill intervention cracks with seeds.

Coratoe blooms falling on good soil will root.
        The dry stem, lightweight yet strong,
                acts as a centre beam for a Maypole jig.

It is another Sunday morning.
        I hear a clamouring and know that, in an unnamed
                house, cracks appear. A hummingbird sings

till another homing bird finds the good seed of Sunday.
        After a decade of containment, I look to the hills.
                I hear a host of golden Zion flowers singing.

NOTES

a aa ac… accidental in "Port Maria", p. 45; *ass-ets,* in "Dancehall Museum, p. 47; and *Yu-day-done* in "Nanny Spirit Travels" acknowledge in attention to form and word-splitting the influence of Kamau Brathwaite, NourbeSe Philip and Shara McCallum.

"African Slave Trade re-storied": p. 27. The poet persona is a woman who decides to journey with John Newton back in time. She invites readers to join her, standing by Newton's side at the helm of history. She witnesses Newton wrestling with both slavery and his new faith while overseeing the fate of trafficked Africans aboard the *Brownlow*.

agave or coratoe: in "Zion, Where Sea Meets Sky", p. 85. The agave or coratoe is a succulent introduced into southern Europe around the middle of the 16th century and is now naturalized as well as widely cultivated as an ornamental plant, as it is in the Americas.

almond tree: in the poem "Nanny's Pot", p. 39, the tree alludes to a watchfulness that is central to the story in Jeremiah, chapter 1 (New International Bible) that also references wrath, akin to the wrath of God, that is poured out on rebellious people from a boiling pot.

Arawak: in "Fragile", p. 59. As "Jamaica Global" documents, Jamaica was "initially inhabited in approximately 600 AD or 650 AD by the Redware people. By approximately 800 A.D., the second wave of inhabitants arrived – Taínos (Arawak and Caribs). Early historians believe that by 1602, the Arawak-speaking Taíno tribes for the most part had been destroyed. However, recent studies reveal that a few Taínos escaped and thereafter occupied the forested mountains where they coexisted with runaway Africans who had been enslaved."

Blood-dimmed cries, in "John Newton's Thoughts of the African Trade Re-storied", p. 27, alludes to W.B. Yeats's "The Second Coming".

Buck-toe stone: the poem, p. 40, was inspired by the article titled "Quao the Invisible Hunter", by Paul H. Williams, published in *The Gleaner*, about a stone historically connected to the Maroons, on which a contemporary person had stubbed a toe. My father, John Minott, was born in Spring Hill Portland. He is the link to my Maroon heritage.

Cemis / Zemis: In "Lignum Vitae", p. 7, and "Taínos' Zemis Held Captive for Safe Keeping", p. 18. These were sacred wooden carvings that many believed were made from trees containing the spirit of a dead Cacique, a Taíno chieftain.

"Colour I Dancehall", p. 51. The Jamaican artist Ebony Patterson investigates history and its complexities, including the high body count of inner-city youth in Jamaica and Brazil. Patterson explores difference through colour, skin, fabrics, shapes, accessories, plant stems and blooms.

covid-crawl spaces, in "Mapping the Politics", p. 41, alludes to Deborah Lupton's *COVID Societies: Theorizing the Coronavirus Crisis* (1922).

"Dancehall Museum", p. 45. The final line gives a nod to Linton Kwesi Johnson's "Top Notch Poet".

fufu, in "Making Fufu", p. 76, is a pounded, dough-like food made from yam or plantain, found in West African and Caribbean cuisines. The title refers to a painting by Kapo, or Mallica Reynolds, a famous Jamaican artist.

Grief makes us all vulnerable to light: in "Mapping the Politics", p. 41, alludes to James Baldwin's reflections on suffering and transformation, such as in *The Fire Next Time* (1963).

Herodotus. In "A Word from Herodotus (440 BC)", p. 22, I connect the image *of Henrietta Marie,* a slaver and the life of Herodotus, the circa 4th Century BC Greek historian, described variously as the "father of history" (or "the father of lies", because he mixed fact with myth). Telemachus is, of course, Ulysses' son, who sets out on his mother Penelope's behalf to search for his missing father.

Ignatius Sancho. In "Ignatius Sancho Travels on Nobody", p. 20, Sancho (c. 1729-1780) speaks in three distinct voices in the retelling of his birth. He is known for the elegance of his standard English in *The Letters of the Late Ignatius Sancho, an African* (1782). Here, even more than the Caribbean Creole voice, the African voice is the most subdued. "*Mo wa* (Yoruba – *I have come*), *ndinabwera* (Chichewa/Nyanja – *I came*) represent his African voice. He was born on a slave ship, name recorded as unknown. I have named it *Nobody* as a nod to Derek Walcott's poem "The Schooner *Flight*", where his speaker, Shabine, declares: "I have Dutch, nigger and English in me,/ and either I'm nobody, or I'm a nation." (*Collected Poems 1948-1984*, p. 150). It also alludes to V.S. Naipaul's "heretical" statement that Caribbeans have created "nothing" and therefore Caribbeans are nobodies.

I-self, I-selves, in "*Marie Seraphique* of Nantes", p. 15, is a version of Rastafaian Dread talk, recognising Caribbeans who are on a journey to claim self / selves.

It is/ It is a task…, in "Those Who Came After", p. 42, alludes to the beginning of Kamau Brathwaite's poem "Negus" in *The Arrivants* (1972).

It tells me nothing in "The Ships That Scattered Us", p. 12, resounds with the quarrel over Caribbean history that took in V.S. Naipaul, Derek Walcott and Kamau Brathwaite.

Kabisa, Kuwa in "Proclamation…", pp. 56-57 mean, respectively, *absolutely* and *become* in Swahili.

know that the south declines towards/ our place in the setting sun: Aethiopia.
In "Word from Heroditus, p. 21, these lines paraphrase Heroditus
Book 3, line 114, as in <https://shekereblog.wordpress. com/print-
editions/the-blameless-aethiopians> [accessed 24 May 2025].

livity: in "Foreign Policy Writer", p. 72, is a word made popular by
Rastas; it speaks to life, and wellness.

"Mapping Maroon Territory", p. 48. Credit to: Jada Benn Torres
and ResearchGate, adapted from earlier image 1992. The related
online adapted image shows the location of Maroon Towns in
Jamaica. <https://www.researchgate.net/figure/Map-showing-
former-and-present-day-Maroon-settlements-Source-Adapted-
from-Bilby-1992_fig1_323231208 [accessed 5 November 2023].

"Marie Séraphique of Nantes", p. 15, names a French slaver which sailed
from Le Havre to French Equatorial Africa, then on to St. Domingue,
trafficking Africans. Le Havre's history was intertwined with slavery
from the mid-seventeenth century. Slavery received official approval
in Le Havre with the setting up of the Company of Senegal in 1678
to take over the slave trade from the Dutch West Indian company.
Details, credit to Manifest: <https://www.projectmanifest.eu/the-
marie-seraphique-a-slave-trading-ship-from-nantes-in-the-18th-
century-en-fr/ >.> [accessed 28 October 2023]

moder-tongue, in "Ignatius Sancho Travels on *Nobody",* p. 19, is a
nod to Nourbese Philip's reconstruction of language in *She Tries
Her Tongue, Her Silence Softly Breaks.*

Mpoto abwelele; Moto! Moto!, in "Nanny's Pot", p. 39. It translates as
Pot draw them out; Fire! Fire!

"Nanny Sleeps Under a Broom Tree", p. 43. Credit to Desert
Southwest Conference, online blog 1 July 2019. The photo of
a broom tree references the Bible story of Elijah in 1 Kings 19.

Nancy Cushman's interpretation of the passage says, "God meets us in the desert times of our lives, gives us relief like a broom tree...".

"Nanny Spirit Travels", p. 46: the term "lionheart" gives a nod both to King Richard the Lionheart, as a synonym for bravery, and to Sistren's *Lionheart Gal: Life Stories of Jamaican Women*, edited by Honor Ford-Smith.

"New Britannia" was inspired by the image of the ship of that name, and also the events on board prior to the explosion that sank this English slaver. I imagined Kamau Brathwaite in conversation with Bijago fathers, a group from what is now Guinea-Bissau.

'Pinta, Niña and Santa Maria': in "La Santa Maria", p. 13, and "Penning Down Possibilities", p. 30, the three ships that Columbus set sail with on his first expedition.

Port Maria was inspired by an investigation of a ship that sank on a return voyage from Jamaica to London, 30th Jan 1773. Port Maria the town where Mama Ignota acquired her first home as a young woman. Ignota is the granddaughter of Katherine Henry (a Taíno ancestor) whose daughter Ethel, was fathered by the son of Maas Edward, otherwise known as Busha. In the poem, the stuttering words allude to M. Nourbese Philip's poem *Zong!* (2008) and a performance of that poem.

Prospero and Caliban: in "A Prayer for Ships that Scattered Us", the story of Prospero and Caliban, which first appears in William Shakespeare's *The Tempest*, was used by the Barbadian author, George Lamming, in *The Pleasures of Exile* (1960) as the archetype of the relationship between coloniser and colonised. The quote, "We learn Prospero still fears Caliban", comes from Lamming. Other Caribbean writers who have used *The Tempest* as an archetype of colonial dynamics include Aimé Césaire, Roberto Fernández Retamar, Elizabeth Nunez and Derek Walcott.

"Rascals, rogues, freebooters": in "Penning Down Possibilities", p. 30, refers to Winston Churchill's infamous comment: "Power will go to the hands of rascals, rogues, freebooters; all Indian leaders will be of low calibre & men of straw." It is interesting to think that recent leaders in the United Kingdom include Humza Yousaf, a Scottish politician who served as First Minister of Scotland and Leader of the Scottish National Party from 2023-2024; Sadiq Khan as mayor of London from 2016 to the present; and Rishi Sunak, former prime Minister of the United Kingdom 2022-2024.

"Recovery": this poem was inspired by a *caricature* by Isaak Cruikshank of the image of a young girl strung up on the deck of a slaving vessel. The print was presented by the plaintiff in the case against John Kimber as evidence of the inhumane treatment on the merchant ship *Recovery*. - 2nd April 1792.

Slavery Abolition Act 1833: See "Proclamation", p. 65. https://www.legislation.gov.uk/ukpga/Will4/3-4/73/1991-02-01/data.pdf.

specterrific, in "Nanny Spirit Travels – Suppliant Sisters", p. 46, is a coined word previously used by Greg Pardlo.

"Spirit of Jonkonnu Reach the Lane": the poem of that name, p. 49, has as its epigraph a nod to Fae Ellington talking about old-time Jamaican Christmas. <https://www.youtube.com/watch?v=vgAJQPpAByyg> [accessed 25 May 2025].

suppliant sisters: in "Nanny Spirit Travels", p. 46, the suppliant sisters" beg Zeus and other gods to help them through their hardships and to protect them. They escaped Egypt in search of freedom.

Sycorax in "*Marie Séraphique* of Nantes", p. 15 is a nod both to Shakespeare's *The Tempest* and to Kamau Brathwaite's creation of a graphic style and language.

Taíno deities: "Lignum Vitae", p. 7, references the fact that "In April 1799, three wooden figures, said to be Taíno deities, were transported from Jamaica during colonial times. Later they were put on display before the Society of Antiquaries of London, as recorded in its journal ARCHAEOLOGIA in 1803".

Telemachus: See Herodotus.

The Master's tools will never dismantle the master's house, in "New Britannia", p. 17, refers to Audre Lorde's radical perspectives on standard English language, in the collection of essays of that title (2018).

the sea – at first a frivolous emerald green – is forced to grow up into cobalt: in "A Prayer for Ships That Scattered Us", p. 12. This salutes George Lamming's phrase "the sea is cobalt, changing frivolously to green" in *The Pleasures of Exile*, p. 17.

time is challenging us: in "Mapping the Politics", p. 41, relates to the similar theme in Toni Morrison's *Beloved* (1987), where time plays a crucial role in shaping memory and trauma.

"Who Will Tame the Sirens?", p. 24. The Sirens join /extend the quarrel between Penelope (Ulysses' wife) and Calypso (the side chick) staking their claim. The poem references my poem "Penelope to Calypso" in *Zion Roses* and "Calypso" in *The Water Between Us* by Shara McCallum. The Sirens have special powers, capable of controlling winds and waves and of circumventing well laid plans.

X-Self, X/Self: is the title of a collection of Kamau Brathwaite's poetry published in 1987. The term refers to a fragile and alienated self that is yet to be discovered. I-Self is derived therefrom.

Several poems in section 1 have been influenced by the scholarship and cultural politics of Kamau Brathwaite. Discussions of "Nuum by Raad Kareem Abd-Aun and Sabrina Abdul kadhorn Abdulridha offer a new perspective.

ABOUT THE AUTHOR

Winsome Monica Minott is a chartered accountant and poet. Her second poetry collection *Zion Roses* was longlisted for the 2022 OCM Bocas Prize for Caribbean Literature, and she has received two awards in the Jamaican National Book Development Council's annual literary competitions for book-length collections of her poetry. She was awarded first prize in the inaugural Small Axe poetry competition. Her poems have been published in *The Caribbean Writer*, *Small Axe Caribbean Journal*, *Cultural Voice Magazine*, *SX Salon*, *Jubilation*, *Coming Up Hot* and *The Squaw Valley Review*, and more recently in *BIM* magazine. Some of her poems have been broadcast on Power 106 in Jamaica. Her debut collection, *Kumina Queen,* was published by Peepal Tree Press.

A STATEMENT FROM THE COVER ARTIST:
STEFANIE THOMAS GILBERT-ROBERTS

Titled **Celestial Crossings:**

A crimson moon rises over an indigo sea.
Bronze specks scatter across the deep blue.
Luminous traces of journeys remain ever present.
Inspired by Minott's poetics of deconstruction,
decolonial reclamation through ekphrastic dialogue.
Memory exists not in fixed lines,
but in echoes, fragments, and tides.

ALSO AVAILABLE

Kumina Queen
ISBN: 9781845233174; pp. 68; pub. 2016; £8.99

This is an accomplished and pleasing first collection. Poem after poem make us sit up and think, sometimes smiling at the low-key irony, as we follow the variety of personae and topics. One of the striking areas of interest is the poet's imaginative projection of the African heritage of Jamaicans, and, in this regard, her subtle use of folk beliefs and idiom. – Edward Baugh

Cultural inheritance is a recurrent feature in this rich collection. The title poem presents a persona "schooled in containment" who wishes to skip over generations keeping her in, and "dance the dance" of an earlier ancestor. Celebrating the range of Jamaican language... the poems explore "an ache coded / in the bloodline"; they often refer to family and female figures in African Jamaican history or legend... who have confronted challenges. In various shapes and voices, many of the pieces also reflect cosmopolitan experience, revising classical myth... This is an impressive book. – Mervyn Morris

Zion Roses
ISBN: 9781845235178; pp. 72; pub.2021; £9.99

Zion Roses, with its alluring title, builds impressively on the promise of Minott's *Kumina Queen*. The pursuit of self-realisation runs through inter-related themes such as family, ancestors, the challenges of a girl's growing into womanhood, and these grounded in the history of African-Jamaican slave experience. She engraves Jamaican folk culture in her word-scape, as in the sequence that revives "jonkunno", the theatre of the streets. Art and music become integral parts of the experience, as in the poems about Jean Michel Basquiat, Paul Gauguin and trombonists Don Drummond and Rico Rodriquez. The title poem, which closes the collection, is a song of praise, instinct, in the nuances of the title itself, with the issues explored in the preceding range of poems. The Zion of Christianity interplays with Rastafarian, and "Roses" illuminates each. – Edward Baugh